A DIFFERENT ME
SOCIALLY AWKWARD

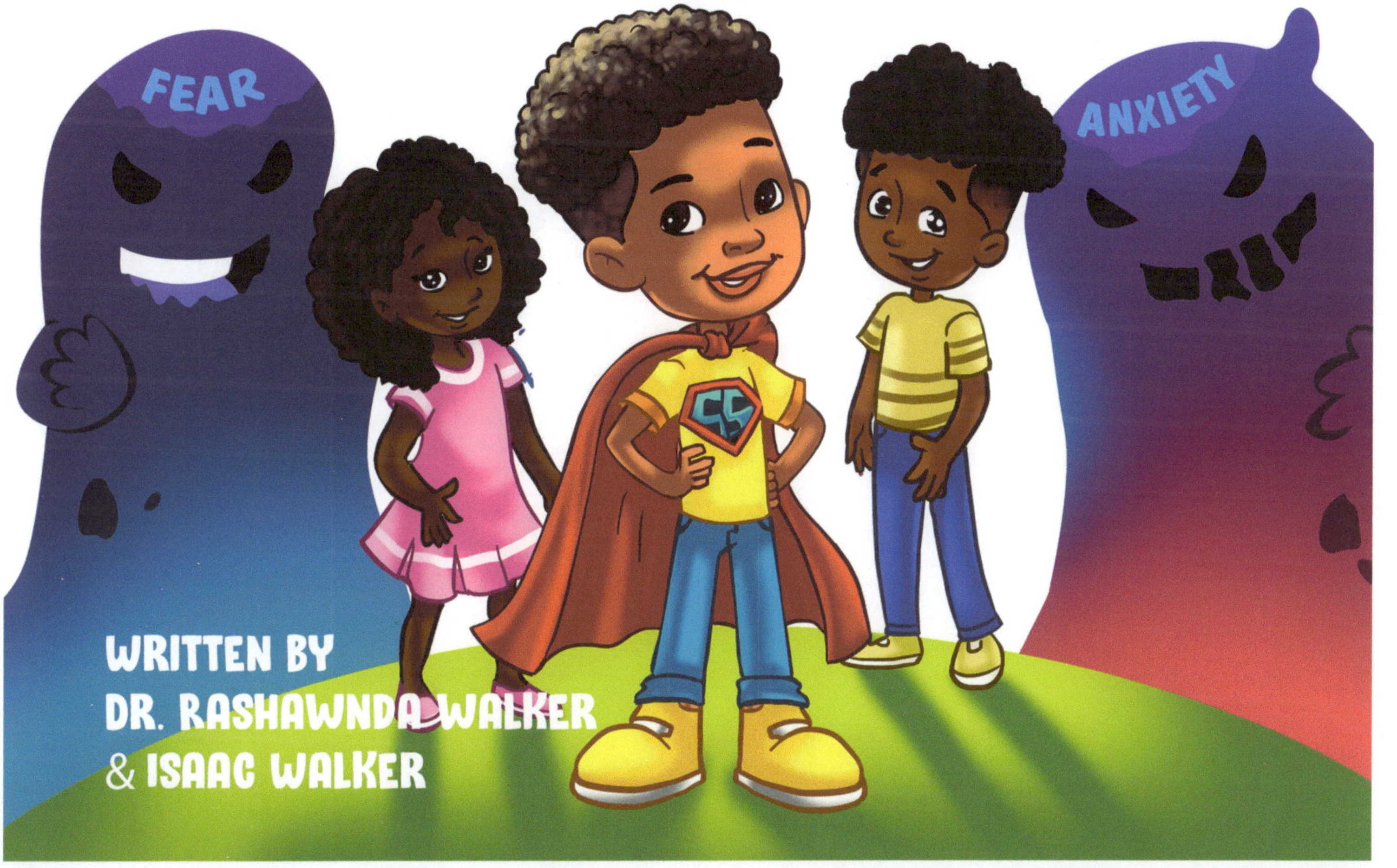

**WRITTEN BY
DR. RASHAWNDA WALKER
& ISAAC WALKER**

A DIFFERENT ME:
SOCIALLY AWKWARD

A DIFFERENT ME : SOCIALLY AWKWARD
© 2023 Dr. Rashawnda Walker

All rights reserved. This book or parts thereof may not be reproduced in any form, stored in a retrieval system, or transmitted in any form by any means—electronic, mechanical, photocopy, recording, or otherwise—without prior written permission of the publisher, except as provided by the United States of America copyright law.

ISBN: 979-8-9891011-0-8

This book is dedicated to any kid who has turned awkwardness into awesomeness...

My funny looking face is all they see. Maybe it's my hair that makes me look different because my curls are weird. Are they matted?

My skin is brown, but maybe it's too light. Or... is it too dark? I always feel I don't look right. I just look... different.

I want to talk to people. I just wish I knew how, but I don't know what to say or even how to say it.

Will I sound silly?

Will they run away?

Will they laugh at me like I'm some big joke?

What will they think?

They're getting closer. I wonder what they want. They probably don't really want to be friends with me. Or do they? I really want to hide just to be safe. Maybe if I don't look at them, they won't see me.

You see, I think people just don't like me. My mom takes me to a therapist who has a name for how I feel. He understands me. I wish I was talking to him now. What was the name for how I'm feeling? What was it?

Ahh, that's it! He called it social anxiety. It means I get nervous when it's time to talk to people that I don't know.

When they speak to me, I feel embarrassed. Sometimes I feel like they judge me before they know me.

SOCIAL ANXIETY

My therapist gave me a skill to use when I begin to feel this way. He tells me to ask myself what I can do to make myself feel better. I've got it! I have to stop and think about what's happening...

Just because I feel like someone doesn't like me doesn't mean my feelings are true. My affirmations also help me get through. I am enough. I am likable. I am not weird.

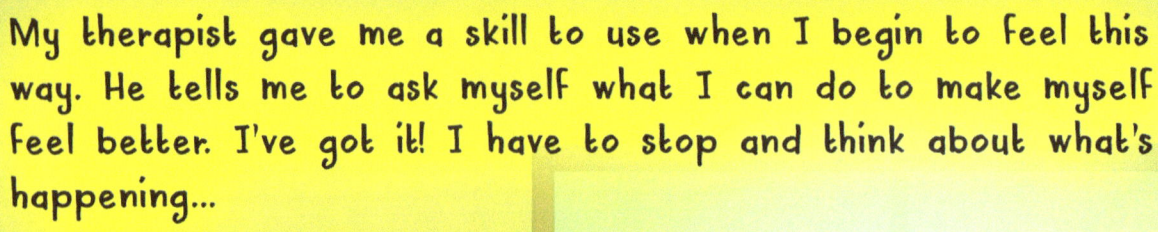

What if they think I look nice? I guess I shouldn't assume they think I look weird. Besides, no one even said that.

Hmmmm... What if they want to be friends? I'm very nice, and other people like me. My mama always says, "Isaac, you're a dope little dude."

I'm funny, smart, and I guess I am dope or cool or whatever... Yeah! They just might like me.

Okay! Now I'm going to blow the breath out like I'm blowing through a straw for six seconds. That's helping...
The good thing is that I can do it as much as I need to until I feel ready and steady.

I walk up to the group with my head held high and my chest out. "Hi," I say nervously.

The boys smile and one of them says, "Hi! We need a fourth player. Can you play with us?"

I can't believe my ears. Someone really wants to play with me! "Yes. Yes!" I exclaim. Another boy from the group says, "Good because we really needed one more person. For a second, we thought you wouldn't want to play with us. Let's do it!"

We had a blast playing together. I'm so glad I didn't let social anxiety stop me from being brave. Now I have three new friends. What if I didn't speak to them? Sometimes my brain tells me things are worse than they really are. I don't like that, and I'm glad I have tools to help me.

Now I know that I can stop my thoughts in their tracks. If I start to think the worst, I can tell my brain that I know better. Then, I can change that thought into something more positive. I have the BRAIN POWER to beat Social Anxiety! You can just call me a Social Superhero!

About the Authors

Isaac Walker is an eleven year old, 6th grader who loves Super Mario and Spiderman. He also enjoys Boys Scouts, running, football, and Tae Kwan Do. Isaac's goal for telling his story is to help other children who feel different to realize they are not alone. He wants to share his coping skills with others so they can become masters of their emotions just as he is learning.

Dr. Rashawnda Walker has a Doctorate degree in Pyschology with a focus on Clinical Psychology. She currently practices as a Licensed Professional Counselor, proudly serving military, first responders, and civilian communities alike. She provides mental health evaluations and counseling services. Dr. Walker's special areas of interest include adults, adolescents, and children with depression, anxiety, and other areas of intense psychopathology. Other areas include ADHD, Autism Spectrum Disorders, school learning, and conduct problems along with other developmental conditions.

Dr. Walker's goal, inspired by Isaac's struggles, is to bring awareness to the mental health struggles of African American children to light and to give subtle interventions through their love of reading.

Social Anxiety Guide

Social Anxiety (SAD) is persistent fear of social interactions or situations that require social performance in which a person may be subjected to scrutiny by others (American Psychiatric Association, 2022). Children fear negative evaluation during these interactions. When the fear is persistent, it can affect their daily life and functioning. Social anxiety is normal and almost expected in children, especially teenagers. Everyone feels anxious or worry from time to time, but the problem occurs when the anxiety is disproportionate to the situation. This guide is designed to help parents, caregivers, teachers, and other people children encounter recognize and help a child through their anxiety, maximizing their social potential during the important developmental years. We hope to encourage caregivers to reach out to mental health professionals for guidance and coping techniques as there are many reasons children may feel socially anxious. As always, early intervention is the best.

Some ways to recognize social anxiety in a child include:

- The child may be withdrawn in social situations, fear being the center of attention, or fear embarrassment in social situations.
- The child may appear awkward in typical situations (i.e., parties, recess, small groups, etc.).
- The child may be considered "shy" when they encounter strangers, people they do not know very well, or in general.
- Physical signs may be sweating, wringing hands, irritability, leg swinging or tapping, nail biting, hunched shoulders, or an overall awkward posture. Pulling hair or hair missing in patches or small inconspicuous sections may indicate a more prevalent anxiety problem.
- The child may be self-critical after social interactions with other children. For example, the child could have a typical interaction with another child, but they will consistently rehash the events and may say phrases like, "Did I sound stupid?" or "I wish I wouldn't have said that."

Here are a few questions related to Isaac's interactions in this book to invoke candid conversation about anxiety with a child.

- Who was the antagonist?
- What did Isaac think about himself?
- Were Isaac's thoughts true? How do we know?
- What did Isaac do to master his fear?
- What happened to Isaac in the end?
- What would happen if the other children did not want to play? What could Isaac do?
- Have you ever felt like Isaac? If so, when? Did you get through it? If so, how?
- How often do you feel like Isaac?
- How can you become a Social Superhero?

References:

American Psychiatric Association. (2022). Diagnostic and statistical manual of mental disorders (5th ed., text rev.). American Psychiatric Association Publishing.

www.ingramcontent.com/pod-product-compliance
Lightning Source LLC
LaVergne TN
LVHW072116070426
835510LV00002B/85